FLORA/FAUNA

VOLUME ONE

to Jean & Arthur

Published in the UK and internationally by Open Shutter Press

Web: openshutterpress.com
Instagram: @petetaylorpoetry
Email: editor@openshutterpress.com

ISBN: 978-1-7385177-0-1 (hardcover)

OSP002
First published in 2024 – All rights reserved

Cover artwork – 'Dazzle' by Alex Hadwen-Bennett
@alexhbdesigns

Cover design by Andrew Morgan of Morgan Creative
@morgancreative_

Interior layout by Pete Taylor
@petetaylorpoetry
Typeset in Perpetua

FLORA/FAUNA

VOLUME ONE

A Collection of
Nature Poetry & Photography

EDITED BY PETE TAYLOR

OPEN
SHUTTER
PRESS

ANN AVEYARD: *Logol, late king of the Marsh Pride, Masai Mara*

INTRODUCTION

Pete Taylor
Editor
February 2024

No need for me to talk about climate change or endangered species. We all know the score – and the natural world isn't winning. So I'll simply welcome you to the first volume of FLORA/FAUNA, which aims to help people connect with Nature through words and pictures.

To begin in the time-honoured style of anthologists: *In these poems and photographs, we encounter...* all kinds of landscape and seascape, all weathers and seasons, a dozen types of tree, a variety of fruit and vegetation, over twenty species of bird, plus assorted fauna ranging from woodlice to white horses. We hear of a jackdaw in the house and kangaroos on the lawn. We see a wasps' nest, a protest, abandoned footwear and a milkmaid in curlers. What's not to love?

The photography comprises images from professionals and skilled amateurs alike, whose subjects are as diverse as a spider's web and an elephant's tusks. The poetry includes expressions of wonder and desire, awakening and belonging, remembrance and regret.

This work is highly creative and finely crafted. Its purpose is to explore how Nature relates to the many experiences of being human.

A huge thank-you to our contributors – talented people of all ages (from 8 to elderly) and many nationalities, working in England, Scotland, Wales, Ireland, Italy, South Africa, the Philippines and, not least, a dozen different US States.

But since our theme here is 'green', where better to start than on the Emerald Isle itself...

DAVID WRIGHT: *The Bicycle, County Galway, 1980s*

Jane Clarke

INISHBOFIN MEADOW

Behind the fallen-down shed
wild oat grass twists and bends,

restless with meadow-browns
and ringlets. Brambles arch

from a spindle hedge, bearing
berries plump as September.

Marsh thistle threads the field;
purple florets on upright stems.

A breeze blows in from the sea –
timothy sways, quaking-grass

quivers heart-shaped flowerheads
while brome brushes soft as breath

around the leaf-and-stem weave
that shelters ten corncrake eggs.

Reprinted from Jane Clarke's Coracle *(Museum of Literature Ireland, 2023)
by kind permission of the author.*

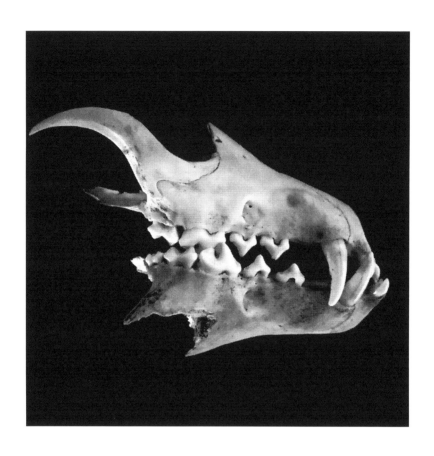

JANE LOVELL: *Dog Fox*

Jane Lovell

FOX SKULL

Fox skull strung in a bag,
the last scrags of fur
wet carpet clumps clung to bone;
his scattered self, the broken china of him
unearthed by wind and rain,
a salt wind ridden by scavenger gulls,
beaks strung with rinds –
      his old flesh, old dog.

He didn't see it coming,
the scowling wind, blats of rain,
his bleared eyes fixed on something
he could no longer reach,
blunt-toothed, belly shrivelled to a root,
confused by the feeble light,
      the slowing of days.

Fox skull submerged in peroxide fizz.
So thin the clean bone,
peroxide bone, petal-thin.
So perfect the sockets of his eyes.
Gone to a crow the worlds glistening
in those orbits,
the nightfall glint that worried sheep,
      startled hare.

Fox skull in a box,
teeth glued in, jaw secured.
Something sculpted from the edge of night:
willow moon, its pits and craters.
Something whipping past leaving only
disturbed air:
dog fox, slipping the wind,
its lightfoot chase through tumps
      of heather.

Jane Lovell

JACKDAW IN THE SPARE ROOM

Snapshot:

his perfect head sharp-cut,
jet black, wet-slicked,
the grey nape velvet,
a bolt of white tin, his eye,

and him trucking like that
behind boxes and old tables
piled with books,
claws scagging the carpet,

his beak, a mollusc
– fossil *orthoceras* –
400 million years of opportunist
spearing and clamping,
roadside scavenging
grume and mash, things stuck
to tarmac.

Life's short
and he knows it.

He's young this one,
compact and ultra-smart.

He eyes me from a dark corner.
There are no questions,
just accusations,
in his pin-sharp tilt.

ANDI SHERRIDAN HOWLEY: *Hawk Eye*

Paul atten Ash

SHINRIN-YOKU
(森林浴)

Beneath wild *kintsugi* skies
I harl up through the ancient King's Wood,
bathed in the calm majesty of oak, ash, sweet chestnut,
soothing into being, I feel this gold-green seep to the core,
the upcast closing in on the West Mendip Way,
the horizon a gilded scar.

On Wavering Down I fly,
a lone raptor rising above the rim of the world,
readying over endless sinking planes, deep in the hunt,
(the husks of creatures mulching unseen into the moor),
to tilt over the brow of the heathland's lost ways,
my heart a flickering star.

Paul atten Ash

THE GIRL IN THE OAK

atop Troopers Hill
my angel of dust ascends
masked in ancient oak

bearing witness
to the choke of the city
its broken ghosts

that have overslept
to wake on this dead rock
extinct: time up

lost in dreams
of tall ferns feathering
Carboniferous skies

still, each night
I will turn out your light
my sleeping angel

yours eternally
the last image I will see
before darkness

before this burden
we have dumped on you
breaks me for good

ROBIN GREEN: *Empty Wasps' Nest*

CHOCOLATE IS PREDICTABLE, WAR IS OBVIOUS
after Susan Sontag

What I like:
Dog-eared paperbacks, homemade rice custard, waves crashing,
obsidian, knowing names of Premier League footballers, bay
windows, wool, handwritten letters, apricots, the word *languid*,
blue gates, afternoon naps in the sun, textiles and tapestry, paths,
the sound of migrating geese, adagios.

What I dislike:
Canned peas, statements posed as questions, the outfield, family
secrets, ice water in winter, mold (except in bleu cheese),
parsimony, horror films, artificial turf, nausea, sloppy editing,
small talk, Velcro, when I procrastinate, wasps, excuses, tyrants.

Di Slaney

DESIDERIUM: WHAT TAUREAN WOMEN WANT

We want more space, newgreen, another
six-acre field. We want softstill, keep
calm voices in our heads, reap
reward from rumination, smother
shiverquakes of rage which make
us flicker into red. We want shy
hearts to beat in slowtime, take
wide breaths that taste of sky
and soil, stay solidtrue to those who
love us and love them back three
thousandfold. We want to see
the ones who pierce us badlyrue
their choices, want our persistence to pay
off, stoutheart patience hardwin us the day.

HOLLY STEWART: *Blyde River Canyon, South Africa*

KERRY BAILEY: *Across the Fields of Barley*

Hylain Rackley

AWAKENING

A glimpse of sunrise
Barley husks rustling softly
Nature's melody

David Lewis

WELSH HILL POEM, 2023

A year now since cold days in dark barns,
Losing daylight through an iron door.

Beyond a hedge reduced to thorn,
A walk of sheep, a falling anger of wrens,
A kite-quartered sky,

And rare moments
Of my mother's smile,
As hill-light over my father
Wondering his water-lanes,
The old roads, his valley-paths.

In his absence I crave his wild spaces,
His dusk-thorn wind-bent
High roads in a half-light;
Our distant, frozen hills.

GABY ZAK: *Clatteringshaws Loch, Dumfries & Galloway, Scotland*

M T Ross

MY NORTH STAR

The North is more than geography
A place on a map
It's a sense of belonging
Something that centres your soul
The air is different
No matter where you go
The people have grit
It's born from hard times
Adversity it seems
Has worked its wondrous charms
For it produces a kinship
A sense of belonging
From sing-song dialects
Rows of houses aglow
Familiar sights
The roads I know
My North is mine
And it's yours
A heart pull
A safe space
A knowing I'm HOME.

Michele Noble

PENNINES

where land meets sky,
clouds brush grass
woven with purple
mats of fragrant time.

Land broods
in the changing weather.
The top bleak peaks
tower over the world
at their feet.
crease deep,
into valleys gridded
with dry stone walls.

Then a drift of white.
The eerie silent flight
of a ghost-white owl

shedding a feather

drifting

dreamily

down

to mark

its passage.

EMMA CATHERINE: *Good Ways and Ancient Paths*

CURBAR

Humble heather and whetstone walks
The paths of the peaks
Root my soul to the earth
Draw the air in my lungs to the sky
Leaning down and in
Stretching up and out
As I stand on the Edge
I am connected to the ground
Feet on solid rock
And I lift my arms up high
Breathing life to my bones
This is my spacious place
This is where I belong

ALENA POLLITT: *Neva Meets Dorothy, Colorado*

Jessica Taggart Rose

NOTES ON MY RELATIONSHIP WITH MOUNTAINS

'that witnessing presence'
— *Denise Levertov*

Higher than clouds that shroud the valleys
I watched sun filtering down
mist burning off
snowdrifts

Air ever so slightly thinner here
I felt gravitas, complexity
clouds shifted quickly
like cares

Riding through Yellowstone snow
geysers shot sulphur through ice,
bacterial pools boiled
yellow

and a wolf lifted its head to watch me pass
a grey wolf, on the mountainside, alone
we shared that moment,
a wisdom perhaps

reverence
for snow
its water
so old
like a
star

Jane Hanson

NO PART IN THE ART

I point the lens
She splays herself before me
Languishing verdant and inviting
Contours rolling ahead
Unspoilt and fresh.
I adjust the focus
She whips up the clouds
And dims the lights
Dips into the paintbox
And paints the backdrop
With a hundred hues
Of scarlet and gold.
The shutter clicks
Everchanging and giving
She generously allows me to stare.
Bewitched by the perfect sunset
Her gifts unique
With no strings
Bounteous nature
My lover.

ANTHONY IBUAKA: *Horizon*

GABY ZAK: *Foggy Woodland Walks*

SOUND SHADOWS
for Truong Cong Tung

You tell a story beyond words
in a forest of trickster shadows.
You touch the rotting rough bark,

a compress into the history
of a dying tree. She perceives the pulse
of the living. Deciphers your

muted memory lodged in your
tangled soul. You create a shroud
of blossoms, vines, roots, and

prayer beads. Hear other gatekeepers
of nature – insects, monkeys, and
tigers. You regard the typography

of birdsong and share around the
campfire the gourd myth about
a human and a fish contained

in a vessel. Water thrums through
the gravity of their rebirth. You dream
of ghosts and ancestors. Their sound

shadows shift the world with
vibrations through the thin veil
of assurance. Peace in the darkness.

Erica Vanstone

SHALLOW TRACKS

Winter rests its weary head
in the lap of spring; the
morning resists her changes.
I feel our ranges of
stayings and leavings like
the park's half-dressed and
uncertain trees. If I go, I
will never understand how
their roots hug the earth, pulling
worth from clumps of mud.
But perhaps these truths
will never be revealed if I
stay—maybe we'd both
remain unhealed, unsafe.
Like the surrounding
sidewalks, a truth unspoken
becomes our prayer: *we're all
a little chipped and broken.*
The question is whether or
not the cracks are deep
enough to make us stumble,
or if they are shallow tracks
others can span without snare.

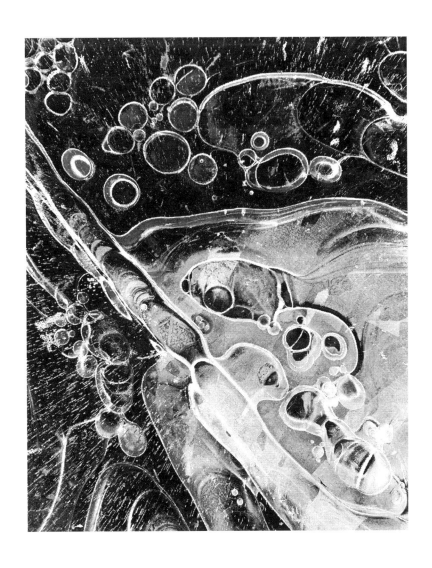

SUSAN SANCOMB: *'Surfacing', ice formation, Chipuxit River*

EMMA CATHERINE: *Frosted*

BROOKINGS

you drive through the forest—roads mostly abandoned—with yellow dotted lines like the sunflower buttons on your son's jacket—expecting to find more green, evergreen—but you turn a sharp corner of the two-lane highway—and suddenly everything is—blue, blue, blue—pale blue sky, cobalt rock, cerulean waves— jagged peaks rising from fine wet sand—a colossal grayed rhino buried to its horns—children make a fine parade behind crabs scuttling to bury themselves—before chubby feet surpass them—a teen girl screams as the cold water overtakes her—the boy laughs— it sounds like a tin can hitting the mesh metal garbage bin—to you who recently lost a lover—the waves now drown out the voices and it's only sea and stones the size of cottages—but slanted like the poor builder was drunk—you long to climb them—but they are steep and slick with saltwater, dirty foam, and bulbous barnacles— persistent in their living together—they will never be alone

Jessica Taggart Rose

WINTER SONG

How the low sun
ignites a boat across the bay,
illuminates tower block eyes,
peeks under horizon:
gold, flicking pink flecks
up to play catch with clouds.

How the smooth blues,
peaches, mauves, myriad yellows
cast a wineglass shadow against
the Whisper White wall:
thumb-smudge muck, salt spray,
dried raindrop projections.

How to name the hues:
dusky rose, apricot kiss, opal, mistletoe
that chalky shallows reflect
while I imprint the scene:
taste of haddock, samphire,
give thanks to fish and sea.

How to sit here
until light dissolves to black
until bats feed in streetlights
until riotous seagulls sleep
until the rising ocean
comes to claim this shore.

ROBIN GREEN: *Snowflake Fall*

ANDI SHERRIDAN HOWLEY: *Mallards Pike Lake, Forest of Dean*

A MEETING IN THE WOODS

The fox dog stood in my path.
His red coat glinting in the weak winter sun.
Dark eyes bored into me
And the tip of his tail quivered –
A landlord, outraged at my trespass,
Poaching his peace of mind.

I stood frozen, my own coat pulled tight around me,
Unwelcome in a world where I did not belong.
Then he turned his back on me, trotted off,
Taking beauty away with him.

There was only empty space where the fox had stood
And loneliness on my walk back home.

ROBIN GREEN: *Saplings through Winter Mist*

Anita Gracey

STILL

The camera lost its focus today
a shutter clicks but nobody moves

codling larvae pause their feast
apples brown on orchard floor

strawberries lose their sweetness
gooseberries gain bitterness

fairy hawthorn still
silent stoic stones

dogs whimper, the kettle keens
primal tea brings little warmth

bell chimes in vain for early mass
overhead crows sing a cheap elegy

an eternity of grey skies
we need a silver hue of light

we breathe in grief
and breathe out

repeat again
again and again

till we become familiar
you are gone.

Joseph Nutman

TAKING A MOMENT WITH TOMAS TRANSTRÖMER

I take my leave of the living room so my love
can listen to a podcast and prepare for her day, there
in a nook of our modest garden that we are blessed to have
I sit on my dusty step, there's a book on my lap

under two lingering grins – one is the moon
in the cool cool abashed blue of space,
giving enough light to read by. After a few pages I give
a satisfied sigh like a tired wave grateful for the beach,

a flock of pigeons abandon their roost in the dying tree,
a clap of their wings seems apt for everything arranged
before the full stop. Then, like the silence draped on
the end credits of a late-night movie,

a buzzard closes the curtain on the moment
with its gliding assassin cut through heaven –
and I notice a cup of tea on the step next to me
that wasn't there a moment ago.

KERRY BAILEY: *Unfolding Lily, Abstract*

SAMANTHA HOOVER: *Dandelion Wish*

Anita Gracey

I DON'T CARE

I don't care for dandelions,
keep them controlled –
I was brought up that way.

Kept them at arm's length
pursing my lips and blowing,
the seeds lift off, snatched by air,
they were told they were ugly,
parachuting down
separated.

You can't turn your back –
I was told.
Their roots sharing blood soil
they would lace your lawn
its faces twisted to the sun
the lion's jagged leaves
swinging on the breeze.

Like being touched by rain
I realised they were wildflowers
surprised from my deckchair
I wake up, crying
my God what have I done.

Frankie Martins

YOUR SONG FALLING

Flat-pack birds' nests tangle with
The desperation of unwashed hair
Begging comfort from a knotting embrace
hoping with each new twisted limb
to be smothered in themselves
beneath, the scuffs of soured leather
are brushed away by droplets
unboiled and ever bulleting
they leave fickle maps shredded and
wrestling with the rotting leaves
your song snaps limp underfoot
its dainty skull made ugly
split open alongside rabbit bones
inquisitive woodlice urged to jump
by its empty socket affirmations

when, inevitably, the clouds decay
into a fungal asphyxiation of the light
and our eyes are cast from hedonism
teeth will chip on starving teeth
tongues will bloat like footsteps
it is in this vain and brutal kiss
that we make casualties of
spring's sun-christened lambs
their spines snapped and wilting
in their shadow a new taste forms
at last, "goodbye" will cower in my throat
instead, I rigidly exhale your title
as if a name could die without guilt
as if it could kill with
the innocence of a mother

ELIZABETH LUKÁCS CHESLA: *Fungi*

TRISH MORGAN: *Reclaimed*

Akash Pillai

HIDDEN HUES

My mother planted a jasmine sprig
It may grow and flower next spring.
My father watered it, patiently, dutifully
for the beauty, it will soon bring.
My grandmother tilled the soil;
She crooned sweet tunes to the buds.
But when they opened out soft
the garden brimmed bright
but not with fragrant white floods.

As the blooms came out,
each a decadent pink
my mother cried into her palms,
and my father looked away pained;
my grandmother died unable to bear
that what they cared for — they raised,
was a rosy oleander disgrace
not the fragrant white jasmine they praised.

God, why did you do this to us?
And my father crushed underfoot,
and tried to uproot,
and tore apart the shrub.
Once regret came,
and they pointed blame,
the damage could not be undone.

HELEN AITCHISON: *Memorial Rose Bush*

Helen Aitchison

MARY'S ROSE

The rose bush grows in my garden,
Bigger each week, month, year,
Like the distance between us.
As cherished memories of you fade,
Becoming somewhat translucent,
Iridescent around the edges,
As they fray, retreat, dissolve.
New thoughts nudge them further away,
Not through significance, just the necessity of life.
But your rose bush keeps strong,
Robust and beautiful, as you were.
How you remain in my mind,
An image that never will fade.
Even when weakened by fragility,
You were still protection and strength,
Like the branches and buds of the rose bush.
The yellow flowers bloom, a buttery magnificence.
Clustered together, creating swirls of fragrant silk petals,
That feel like your hands in ageing years.
This winter, the yellow roses grew,
They bloomed, even in early December,
Lone flowers, thriving against the elements.
Your roses stood tall, just for a few weeks,
And each time I glanced at them,
They comforted me, like a squeeze of your hand.
Your favourite flowers, now mine.
The yellow rose bush, that grows all year round in my garden,
Reminds me you're never far away.

STILL LIFE WITH A SATSUMA

I imagine glass houses
light and luminous,
the gentle hands separating the leaves
and then orangeness.

Now i'm realising
your trees had sunlight
resting dimple-warm.
Rain touched you,
feather breezes, before

this dull green patina;
floured atoll.
A stamped circle in the fruit bowl
before the recycle.

JANE HANSON: *Persimmon*

MARC BESSANT: *Dark Wood*

Jonathan Chibuike Ukah

THE SONG OF A TREE

I was born in the thick forest of Umuegwele,
the home of Opurudu, the coppice masquerade,
the petty god of the black and gold python,
who stands tall and stinks like the Egyptian pyramid,
inhabited and breathless through the carcass of stars,
swallowed in fear, their flesh the slimy syrup of a god;
I know I must shut my door to the wicked spirits
and allow the benign birds to suck my juices,
I am by nature of intense hospitality cursed
and cannot alter my destiny by style or design.
Birds build their nests on my teetering leaves,
while insects and flies perch on my boughs and pines,
when the Harmattan sends pelting winds of pebbles;
or the day turns cloudy with lightning threatening;
often does the sun pierce through the veins of leaves,
to warm insects and worms made desolate by rain
and pollinate the flowers awaiting a rebirth,
when the spirits of the land show no grace.
The sucking flies stay, hiding within my folded nooks,
while birds shelter and shield within my crooked elbows.
When in bloom, I wear a hat of billowing leaves,
green, yellow, gold or grey and black canopy;
that's when I ascend closer to the laughing stars,
that send me to light and bless me with a thrush smile,
which guides me through this darkening wood.
Without ecstasy, I welcome the death of every season
and rejoice when it's time for them to grow and glow again;
though the sun acknowledges me with its sharp rays,
it could carry my heart-wrenched tears to Heaven,
when the grips of cruelty wind up around an axe,
lashing me to shreds, to cold molecules uncut.

JAKE SPENCER: *Woodsman*

BEAUTIFUL BOY AT THE TREE

your skin is sunnysmooth
the bark is roughlydarkling
and your hands have never
grafted anywhere near soil
never broken ground never
felt earth siltfill your nails
such prettypretty nails on
your languidlovely hand
offering a long pale flower
s t r e t c h r e a c h i n g
behind the trunk no wider
than your shoulderglories
but so much stronger so
manifestmagnificent
while your lilyrosepeony
all whitewhite in contrast
bows its head to grass for
love for sorrow for joy or
for regret your face hides
what you want to say but
you must say it to the tree
tell the tree tell the tree
before it eats you before it
roots and splits and roots
and splits you suckermad
thirstingtruth like water

Tim Paddock

PREVAILING

Tree screams sky,
bough bent angles point way wind went
branches billow blown buffeted crew cut topped;
by storm barbers spiral isobar stack,
gale gnarled steadfast standing still,
against annual odds root wrangling a place
ever pointing the way of its friend and foe;
bringer of summer rain harbinger of winter squall.
Stand strong angling the way telling summer songs of
    what once hurled across slopes
whistled past stones
sifted chaff dead wooding all weak perished limbs.
Stripping leaf and seed, hurling wide yonder
root trunk bent bough only hold;
tight rings belying true age,
making wood good for a violin to resonate again with wind
    even after long years spent holding

JOE RAINBOW: *Windblown*

JAKE SPENCER: *Natural Curves*

WILD LIFE

I tine turned black gold
saving lob worm friends for pastures new.
Walked tree strewn river wild gravels,
while spotted stream tigers
chased from root branched liars
to harry and smash creations.
Found sea silver wolf packs
hunting, crashing fry
Bass frenzied amid the moonlight.
Watch otter pups holt led,
play with moonshine,
chattering happily gaming tag,
while mum patiently teaches
how, when, where to fish.
Saw star flung meteors
slowfall like fireworks.
Flowering green showering orange
red lumps disintegrated
effervescence across our sky.
Searched far flung sea swells arrival.
Bay bend, crash rocks, build banks
exploding white lines across our shores.
Caught storm clouds bent back;
black rain bearer front
line contoured altitudes sculptured
about a cliff head before landfall
cracked the deluge break.

Joy Wassell Timms

PEDUNCULATE OAK

Cupules spilled – unripe acorns
litter humus rich earth; clenched worlds
opened before their time,

trees forty years old before acorns produced

unready, green-flecked oval cases
capped by bristle shells, I nestle
your prickly cupules in my palm,

peak acorn fecundity is between 80-120 years

read your genome potential,
your star sign, your fate,
dumped in a dead-end wood,
crushed by winter squalls, stamped by boots.

growth slows at 120 years to extend life span

Can you withstand
some random act of kindness?
Shall I push you down the slope,
leave you swaddled under dank leaf mould,
so deep, no squirrel can paw,
– your roots set sail.

Cindy Rinne

THE LANDSCAPE TURNS INWARD

Thoughts of the aspen tree with its wounds—

My lenticels still bleed.

I know my time draws near.

A weakening in my circulation.

Many tried to heal me.

There's a stillness in the fading.

Even a goddess experiences loss.

One day the yellow birds will sing in new branches.

Empyrean will find warmth.

PAUL MORRIS: *Snowshadow*

Erica Vanstone

WINTER-FLOWERING CHERRY

His grief is a twisted tree
with iced, dark branches.
Every flowering twig an
Atlas, bravely bent over,
clinging to withered fruit.
Each globe of frozen water,
an anger poised at any
moment to let go.
In December, its drops
are halted, his anguish
becomes suspended;
a string of unmoving
sighs, clear enough for
all to look through.
His grief is a twisted tree,
its stubborn roots clutch.
But somehow, its blossoms
survive—when surrounding
lights are dimmest, it survives.

KELLY SCHULZE: *Ashen November*

Silvia El Helo

TREE

& on one autumn day   all the men I knew
left me   so effortlessly
the tree   stripped of its leaves   its bones
like seeds
& knuckles   still
breathing   *how abandoned*
are you?   & where is
your equivalent?   this tree
exhaling its leaves
like children
born in spring with
no effort

Sylvie Jane Lewis

A ROBIN IN A SCHOOL SHOE

Face up in a leather cot
eyes shut. Two puncture marks
at the heart of the red breast.
Cat fangs. Nearly cold body
resting under the black band.
Tiny feet in the toes. Mine.
My mother wouldn't tell me
until years later that a bird
took my shoes for a grave.
Scooped him out,
carried him to our garden
the burial site. Off I went
to learn of how
some substances fill
the container they're given.
That cramped classroom
did not teach me of things
that refuse to be contained:
a childhood the shape of a bird.

SAMANTHA HOOVER: *Lonely Sparrow*

Martin Coldrick

A LARK'S TALES
Embleton, Northumberland, April 2023

Spring lark fizzes like a lit fuse.
Flitting, floating, helium-light,
near-exploding, extolling
the joys of life. High:

a tiny darting dot of dust.
A black speck rising in wide-screen sky.
Bursting – like an over-excited child –
to tell, re-tell and tell again
its tales at double-treble-speed
to anyone who'll listen

and won't still its tattling tongue
or thrumming wings
until it's done, as
innocents expect one and all
to care in equal measure.

STILL WINGS

You had long since passed
By the time I did
Dreams of flight instantly dashed
Against a wall you could not see
I helped you into the air one last time
Carried you to the shelter of a tree
A final resting place in dappled shade
More dignified than the busy roadside.
Shining onyx eyes now dim and greyed
A pointed beak closed up tight
There'd be no more songs at dawn
Celebrating the end of night
A thin summer breeze stirred
Intricate patterns on your tiny form
Whispered over you some parting words
Finding some way to contrive
A final moment where you seemed alive.

RACHEL BERARDINELLI: *Green Heron in Central Park*

Andy Dalgleish

CORMORANT

Cormorant, beaked eel,
all queries done you take a stab

emerging at some distance, sleek,
where oceans of September roll like glass,
to skewer air with earnest new enquiry.

Oh how I envy your fluidity in shifting tides,
submerging days of roil and hurl
when kelped or bashed on rocks.

For you the surf cliffs seem
to swash across and dissipate
with just one shake; then launching late

all neck for land, you will your flight
with rapid wing-beats dwindling —
perchance the glint of silver in your bill.

Elaine Desmond

EYED

A rook watched me
watch a cormorant
tail-flit down to water.
An unsettled arrival:

hesitant and disturbed,
it lifted off low
with tick-tuck
flap to Dooneen Rocks.

Tar-glossed, full span
the cormorant crucifix
wind-bathed while sealight
bristled between dolloped islets.

I turned and saw a cow
watch us all, limpid-eyed,
turn her head away
and bend to grass.

MARCO TIBONI: *Skomer Puffin*

JAMIE SMART: *A Symphony of Motion*

Kristina Diprose

MURMURATION

On the Island of Coll there are starlings
whose song is a two-stroke engine,
little mimics of cold start and judder
who've never met the first speaker,
the ancestor fluent in combustion
whose throat was a piston,
nor do they suspect the rusty wreck
long stuck in the mud is the wretch
who taught him. Others are car alarms
or clattering heels in the dark
or hawk cries or enemy shelling.
They gather as the nights draw in,
shining like oil slicks, to play at falling
and to keep each other warm.

RACHEL BERARDINELLI: *Great Blue Heron Floating*

Jaqi Holland

MIGRATION

Lonely V of stragglers
skimming the spring sky.
The bulk of the flock, a dart,
fled in fall, bullseyed
on an inland marsh due south,
a week's worth of winging
to the great green lip
lacing the coast—Carolina—
landing where their bodies
and poles pointed them,
surprised every time
they hit the mark,
home.

ANN AVEYARD: *Two-Tone*

HOLLY STEWART: *Leopard Eyes*

Jess Challis

THE SWELL

in the place where ancient people slept in slots
along ridges spaces hollowed by a river eons
gone and wrote their stories on red rock
walls I try to sleep while the frogs sing
I lie awake kept alert by the ethereal
sound sprawled atop my sleeping
bag too hot for covers I'm sweating
still wondering how many times did someone sleep
in this place did they fall asleep to the frog
cacophony or are these strange creatures
new from the recent rain the canyon walls rise
higher higher almost to the sky now filled
with millions of stars small white radiating
spots like the eyes of the mule deer
in the beam of my flashlight the wriggling
tadpoles live in muddy puddles
dark spaces filled with thick water tiny
pools that will shrink tomorrow each day hotter
than the last until they are only crusted
earth the fire is nearly extinguished
like tiny suns the stars set and color rises
in the world again pink now against the flaming
copper cliffs in the growing quiet I go to a puddle
crouching closer my eyes follow a single
tadpole while it glides past
the others life starting anew not
quite a thing yet that will
never live to sing like its mother—

JAMIE SMART: *Head under Water*

TRISH MORGAN: *Essex Skipper in Shropshire*

Christian Ward

THE CRAFTSMANSHIP OF SPINDLE ERMINE MOTHS

Every saran wrapped nettle
is a school of nourishment

for a writhing mass
of caterpillars. Thick as haunted

house mist, the barrier
keeps out ladybirds, green

lacewings and parasitic wasps,
while the caterpillars turn as fat

as corn dogs. The world flips.
They feed. Whatever lesson

is taught here could feed us all.

JULIA CRIPPS: *Gossamer*

Sylvie Jane Lewis

HEDGEPIG

'Thrice, and once the hedge-pig whined'
    – Second Witch, *Macbeth*

Round goblin in the brambles
a beechnut hollowed out
a giant woodlouse or shrunken
armadillo, wandering thistle.

Once, a hedgepig befriended
an old rabbit of ours,
in her last years,
spoke to her through the bars

like a prison boyfriend.
I'd watch them each evening
speak of divination, breakfast,
Wednesdays, being alone, dusk.

DAVID WRIGHT: *Bridie Linnahan milking, Knockgarra, 1990s*

Christian Ward

BRITAIN'S LONELIEST SHEEP

isn't thinking of a whetstone
of a full moon sharpening
the night sky, mountain peaks
stiff like meringues, new-born
lambs marbled in the cold,
the frost's icy breath turning
everything gas-blue, hay bales
dumped like unwanted sofas,
a welcoming barn, the looks
given from neighbouring animals,
tractors doing a scarecrow shift,
a rooster doing its best weathervane
impression. Britain's loneliest
sheep is thinking if it's actually
a sheep at all – not a child
playing dress-up with the seasons,
weather teasing behind the curtains,
a blackbird hiding some unwarranted
sadness in its song.

JON BIDWELL: *Leaves of Grass*

Sylvie Jane Lewis

WHEN OUR GARDEN OUTGREW ITSELF

There were rats in the trees, snickering
in branches that whispered too.
Climbing their beanstalks, they'd conspire,
hatch treetop plans. Slick bodies of silver
messengers to the heavens. Heading high
to dark branches that turn into stairs.
In the air, the clouds open, theatrical
trap doors. The rats laugh
at how they know everything.
How to live anywhere. The rats peer
down on our unassuming house.

Lisa Stone

UNSEASONAL

Flint-heart Winter called today,
And paralysed still-seeming summer:

Hoare frost stole the scent
Of bright geraniums.
The golden marigolds stand frozen,
Iced into a wan submission.
Even antirrhinums pale and bend
Beneath the frosty rime

Which comes too late –
And yet before its time.

TRISH MORGAN: *Nature's Piping*

LORRI SMALLS: *House on a Hill, East Orange, New Jersey*

Holly McKenna

WINTERISING

maybe we'll just talk about the weather,
pretend it's still a smock-donning summer.
the clouds are what we make them after all.

our heads are immortalised in those screens.
overheating on the green, green grass, so
maybe we'll just talk about the weather.

since the rockeries are bare and our eyes
rescinded back to hibernating seeds:
the clouds are what we make them after all,

so let's make them rain just this once for us.
precipitate the contrails early or
maybe we'll just talk about the weather

instead. nod at the window and stare at
our hangnails waiting to bleed. and just
forget when the clouds were what we made them.

after all, we're out of bulbs this season
and the skies have turned to blank papyrus.
there is no weather to speak of any longer,
we can send the clouds back into the sky.

LORRI SMALLS: *Winter Afternoon in Central Park*

Di Slaney

ROOM 154

We hate these walls, all grey then
red so awkward it embarrasses itself.
Smeared panes are sealed. But when
our bodies start to talk, this room

becomes a garden or a field, the grey
is now a seething yield of fertile green,
shoots sprouting up and up as if to say
we grow like you, we grow in you

and leaves wave dappledlime in sun,
loose sap weaves sticky timetrails
through our hair, the taste of fun
is mint and apple crush with texture

on our tongues like tiny caterpillars
wriggling home, pulsing in delight.

Holly McKenna

UNDERFOOT

you are a sweet october, leaving all
too soon. my favourite seasons always walk
the quickest, the orange garnish falling
without a pleasant ending. i must stop
building homes behind unstable ribcages –
their branches are too eager to change –
and i feel my own bones before they break
like twigs. i beg the clearest skies for rain,
but my inner workings do not matter
i'm not meant to last until spring. you sap
the colour from my leaves, watch them scatter
to the wind. and you. searching for untapped
roots as my own turn to whispers, bitter,
as every season leaves them to wither.

SAMANTHA HOOVER: *Discarded Beauty*

ZHOU YANG: *from the 'Faërie' series*

Hylain Rackley

JAPANESE MAPLE TREE

The glory of Fall
An old soul rooted in earth
Luminous scarlet

KELLY SCHULZE: *Great Tisbury Deer*

Kristina Diprose

AT THE WATER'S EDGE

Lorna said she saw three small miracles
from the footbridge we cross every day.
She sent pixelated proof, a ripple
of liquid mammal briefly surfacing.

Jed said the footage was inconclusive.
He reminded me of the time a mink
slunk along the opposite bank
almost otterish enough to fool us.

We once saw a paw print on Mull
fresh enough to bring us back
at dusk to wait at the water's edge
at the neck of a narrow sea loch.

Reb said choose a stakeout spot
near the remnants of a recent feast,
a crab shell cracked on anvil rock
with archaeological precision.

We stayed late in the long June sun
undeterred by biting swarms,
that certain we would see one
if the light stretched thin enough.

Donna Burke Esgro

PAPER BOATS

I am a river
coiling, curving
flowing ore at first light
jumping the reeds, rushes, sedges
trailing silver ribbons of salmon
I run heavy
with blood, tears, poison
broken hearts of bears
wispy with water hyacinths, damselflies

Listen to my ancient songs
from glacial depths
to tarnished surface
Pay heed as I flood, surge, rage
against jagged cliffs
crack boulders and chisel stone
into sacred chasms
Attend as I light the votive candles
of ten thousand transparent spawn
Kneel as you set sail your paper boats
fleeting as wings of time

I am a river
resolute as the constant stars
my blue veins coursing, coursing
to the thumping heart of the sea

KELLY SCHULZE: *Like a Lake of Ink*

SILVIA EL HELO: *Timeline*

SEA SNAIL

sea snails mushroomed at Samar's shores
and children went to the coastline
to gather snails in a basket
basking under the afternoon sun.

lit firewood under a boiling pot
of grated white coconut milk
spiraled shells drenched in liquid
and a pinch of salt sprinkled
mother cooked sea snails.

inside the split-bamboo house
a light from kerosene lamp
circled around a wooden table
shadows behind our backs
the growing family ate together.

those were the times when days
were slow, the nights were long
and the laughter echoed in the room
under a quiet ocean of stars.

BEV CLOUGH: *White Horses of the Camargue*

PAUL MORRIS: *Ainsdale Beach, Merseyside*

Laura Muetzelfeldt

THE LAST TIME WE WERE HERE

Smooth stones under my feet shift
as I move weight from one foot
to the other. The sea is calm today. Careless
waves travel the beach, leaving their
mark upon the pebbles, turning over the small
ones, gently. The sky dark with promised rain.
The dense, rich smell of rotting
seaweed bleeds black ink
into the sand.

It's mild, but I keep
my hand in a pocket, feeling
for the stone you gave me
the last time we were here.
A smirr softly falls. I lift a pebble
shaped like a shark's fin
and a tizzy of sandhoppers
scurry blindly, then melt away
into sand.

EMMA STEELE: *The Marker*

MARY BETH KAPLAN: *Pacifist*

Natalie Wilson

WHITE SAND RECEDING

Waves recede
sand shifts
scooping hollows from beneath my feet
I rock back on my heels
dizzy from
this warm
blue caress

Martin Coldrick

LOW TIDE
Sandsend, Yorkshire, September 2022

Like a fresh crime scene
on infinite repeat,
the sea recedes,
guilty,
from the mess it's made;

slinks into the background,
with sudden innocence,
as if to say, "not me".

It returns, emboldened,
hours later,
wrongdoing undiscovered,
to finish off its unseemly deed,

all the time
sneaking glimpses behind,
ready to skulk away once more.

SUSAN SANCOMB: *'Ascension', tidal pool algae*

EMMA STEELE: *Solitary Beach Hut*

SHALLOWS END
aubade to a beach hut

Long years secure on shingle bank,
at this margin you have lingered
watching how clouds gather,
then breaking, pass.
Memory, through swash of waves unceasing,
has been in pebbles piled up here.

Repaired, repainted every spring
and coolest number in the row,
B-52 now rides the shore.
Revetments gone, rotten past safekeeping,
the stones are dredged
by fetch of storms set free.

Reaching close and closer still our apron,
each tide reshapes the beach.
This time is sooner than foreseen:
the power of backwash –
creating coasts elsewhere –
we never noticed it before.

Donna Burke Esgro

RELICS

In reverence
I gather driftwood
my fingers tracing
the whirl and whorl
of each battered branch

I hold in my arms
vestiges of forgotten forests
coils of desire
vortexes of dreams

I imagine
under the pulsing stars
a bonfire on the shore

Periwinkle sparks
rising
like the wheeling planets
like the shimmer of a mirage
and like
the memory of my wet and sparkling children
waving to me from the brilliance of the sea

MARY BETH KAPLAN: *Bubble Water*

PAUL MORRIS: *Ghost Steps*

WHAT'S LEFT BEHIND

Combing fingers through winkle shells, cowries
and seaglass, she picks out pottery.
In her hand, fragments. Small remnants
of something once whole. She remembers
the beach in Elie, Mum with her trousers
rolled, the sand incongruous against
her bright pink toenails.

Her fingers press the cool, smooth sides
searching for a hard edge
where there is none. She caresses
the shapes – a triangle, a teardrop,
a kite – patterns wearing out, the story
incomplete. Piecing them together
is a puzzle, an attempt to make
something whole. We knew
Mum was dying – now all that's left
is fragments, memories
worn smooth, opaque like seaglass,
still warm in the hand.

Tessa Foley

WARM COCKLES
for Duck Bay, Loch Lomond

They used to say, out here,
You'd be given one minute
to live in that loch
and then you'd be slowed
to an unending hum,
you'd come to a floatstill,
a wrapped, soggy blue,
your face to a mile high
trace of the moon.
And now they say, you!
Come on in, feel the burn,
Like a bathtub with trout,
About time it warmed up,
No more pulling a Leo
when the ripples set in,
still nipples like tin but
you can't ask too much,
Still the Trossachs, y'know,
there is snow on the Ben,
but your heart will still beat,
you'll laugh on the stones
as you step from mellowest
of shallows out here,
the cockles are warmed, and
You'd be given a year to
live under loch and Slate Quay
these here days,
given the heights
of the Holocene age.

EMMA STEELE: *Ice Warning*

SUSAN SANCOMB: '*Ribboning*'

Frankie Martins

IDYLL DECONSTRUCTED

And the sky slashed itself open
Its bleeding ribbons an attempt
To mimic Saturn's rings
Volatile implosion of identity
Froze lava to obsidian
Glinting with youth and
Dusted with so many
Indefinite eyes

My crated bones called it a sunset
Above, the mourners sighed
While god flashed his wealth
They clung to glowing fingers
Stood in awe at the perversity
Of honeyed shadows
Reflecting clouds that
Felt like genesis

There is an insect species
That lays eggs behind the eyes
Of oblivious children
As their laughter bullets upwards
Splitting sunrays with indifferent force
The nativity carves out their pupils
Eyelashes pulling it up
Like a martyr
Years from now, perhaps
A butterfly will die for our sins

NAVILA NAHID: *City by the Sea*

Samantha Terrell

UNTIL THUNDER

The water is still.
I could get lost
In its serenity –
Which is lost
On me today.

But we are not here for the water,
Nor the ancient toppled-over headstones,
In the cemetery next to the ball field –
Which we are, in fact, here for.
At least,

We were.
Until thunder
Brought its own plans.
We did not come for the water,
But the water came for us.

Helen Pletts

IN THE TIME OF FIRES: KANGAROOS ON THE LAWN

they knew we were responsible,
gathering on the clipped-suburban-green
close and dense as kangaroo stalks

that grew each face at the window;
grave and animal. Thirsty, too tired to run

from the flame, they stood and stared
at the brick-forest of human houses
fur-hundreds in their quiet grey-height

DAVID WRIGHT: *Arrested, 'Global Climate Strike', London 2019*

Jessica Taggart Rose

WHAT DO I MOURN?

It's something not quite lost
I mourn not the species gone
gentle summers, nourishing rain
but as we tip over the lip of glass
I mourn the futures we could yet salvage
could be nurturing now.
I mourn our kinder, brighter selves
drowned out.

JESS CHALLIS: *Shadow People*

Holly McKenna

PLAYING WITH SHADOW

i'm playing with shadow, left foot on the
line – existing on the boundary. i
always have a choice, a segment to set
up residence in or to overlook.

i'm playing with shadow, with the dust in
sunlight; hands just waking up after their
prolonged slumber, my unexpectedly
tepid summer stiffening my limbs.

i'm playing with shadow, excavating
previously futile landscapes in the
hope of making them bloom, knowing i can
build wonders upon shaky foundations.

i'm playing with shadow and i'm winning:
each tentative step marked as a triumph.
i live safe in the knowledge that
nobody inhabits the light like i do.

SARAH GARLAND: *The Space Between*

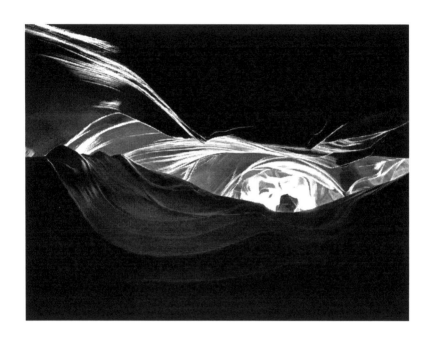

NAVILA NAHID: *Eye of Antelope Canyon, Arizona*

Jaqi Holland

DUSK

A violet haze drapes front porches
slicking triple deckers with twilight,
steam rising from sweetshrubs,
one backyard spilling into the next
in this warm urban valley.

Kitchens and dens lit amber
by moon-powered candles
on a night so thick and still
the crickets chirp, quit.

Not even the moths stir
to circle the porch light
that sputters an apology
before burning out.

SARAH GARLAND: *Blooms of Love*

Michele Noble

AFTER DARK

Midnight.
The garden slumbers,
lulled by the tumbling
song of the weir.

Soft light stretches
the apple tree,
finger-thin, across
dew-lapped grass.

A dreamscape
of velvet shadows.
Shady secrets.

A theatre
hushed,
waiting
for the next performance.

Lisa Stone

GIVE ME THE MOON

Give me the moon
To glow at my breast,
Like a newborn child,
For a time.

Let her nest
In my eyes,
Till the skies
Repossess
What is theirs.

ANDI SHERRIDAN HOWLEY: *Sleeping in the Sun*

CONTRIBUTORS

Helen Aitchison is an author from North-East England. Her writing is inspired by a 20-year social care career and her third novel is due in April 2024. Alongside writing, Helen is director of Write on the Tyne, working with charities to help make creative writing inclusive and accessible. @helen.aitchison_writes | @aitchisonwrites | helenaitchisonwrites.com

Paul atten Ash is the pen-name of Bristol-based Paul Nash. He has been published by Broken Sleep Books, *Butcher's Dog* and *Magma*, among others. Prize shortlistings include: Alpine Fellowship (2023) and Ginkgo (2022, 2021). *Searchlight Seasons*, his debut pamphlet, will be published by Atomic Bohemian in 2024. @north_sea_navigator | @NorthSeaNav | campsite.bio/northseanavigator

Ann Aveyard is a wildlife photographer based in the New Forest, Hampshire. Following a decade as a wedding photographer, she turned to her passion for photographing wildlife, which had begun with her first trip to Kenya in 2011. Ann has won many awards for her photography and hopes her work can help inspire people to prioritise the natural world. @annaveyardwildlifephotography | ann-aveyard.co.uk

Kerry Bailey has a background in both fine art and photography, having studied both at university. Texture and form, inspired by nature, are common themes within her images. Her work has been exhibited and earned her a finalist place in the International Garden Photographer of the Year competition, 2022. @greenandbaileyphoto

Rachel Berardinelli is a nature enthusiast in New York City who enjoys photographing birds, insects and flowers. By day she is a lawyer and, in her spare time, can be found volunteering in the city's parks or hanging out with her cat. She's also a film lover who blogs about movies on her website. @serpent_club | serpent-club.com

Marc Bessant is a photographer from Birmingham, UK, focusing on black-and-white photography. He doesn't worry too much about 'photography rules', but instead aims to capture the mood of the moment – which he hopes will result in images that are in some way visually and emotionally compelling. @marc.bessant

Jon Bidwell is a fine art photographer who specialises in images of fading culture, urban abstraction, vintage automobiles and the natural world, whether witnessed in monochrome or colour. Jon and his wife, Lucy, are both full-time artists and live happily with their dog, Livie-Lou, in Overland Park, Kansas. @jonbidwellphotography | jonbidwellphotography.com

Donna Burke Esgro was born in Santa Monica, California, and brought up by seagulls, eucalyptus trees and the local library. Currently living in the hills near Los Angeles, she is working on several writing projects. When not wandering the City of Angels looking for her wings, she teaches Language Arts – intent on turning as many students as possible into bookworms. @the_writing_harpsichord

Mark Cassidy is a retired radiographer now living in Bury St Edmunds, Suffolk. Writing in the gaps between family, birdwatching and Oxfam books, he reads regularly at local spoken word events. His poems have appeared in various European magazines and anthologies, and may also be found online at markbcassidy.blogspot.com

Emma Catherine, lover of trees, skies, the sea, rainbows and sunsets, lives on the edge of the Peak District writing poetry and taking photos of the natural world at every available opportunity, often with coffee in hand. Her three young adult boys are semi-tolerant of her stopping in the middle of nowhere to marvel at the world! @emmacath14

Jess Challis's poetry, multimedia and artwork have been published in journals such as *Ponder Review*, *Slippery Elm*, *Touchstones* and *Beyond Queer Words*. She won first place in 2019 *Touchstones* poetry, second place in *Slippery Elm* multimedia, and third place in 2023 *Touchstones* poetry. She has received awards for her photography in many art exhibitions. @jessmoxiechallis | jesschallis.com

Jonathan Chibuike Ukah is a Nigerian-born poet living in the UK. His poems have been featured in *The Pierian*, *Propel Magazine* and elsewhere. He won the Voices of Lincoln Poetry Contest 2022 and the Alexander Pope Poetry Award 2023. His poetry collection, *Blame the Gods* published by Kingsman Quarterly, was a finalist at the Black Diaspora Awards 2023. @chibuikeukasoanya | @johnking1502 | Facebook: Chibuike Ukasoanya

Jane Clarke is the author of three full poetry collections, *The River* (2015), *When the Tree Falls* (2019) and *A Change in the Air* (2023), published by Bloodaxe Books – the latter being shortlisted for the TS Eliot Poetry Prize 2023, shortlisted for the Forward Prize for Best Collection and longlisted for the Laurel Prize. She lives with her wife in the uplands of County Wicklow, Ireland. janeclarkepoetry.ie

Bev Clough blends her passion for sports, wildlife and travel into captivating collections of nature and local/international sporting images. Always on the move, her camera is a constant companion during her travels, capturing moments that have graced national sports papers and exhibitions, as well as earning some prestigious awards. @bevcloughphotography | Facebook: Bev Clough Photography

Martin Coldrick was born, bred and educated in Yorkshire, where he now works as a journalist. He never intended to start writing poetry and freely admits that both he and his poems are 'works in progress'. Martin uses poetry as therapy – and his writing may be personal or may simply revel in the natural world. These are his first published poems. @theaccidentalexile | accidentalexile.com

Julia Cripps is a mixed-media abstract artist working in the painting, photography and poetry fields. Born in a village in Essex, Julia raised a family and made a life-changing move to live in Canada, before eventually returning to the UK in 2009. See more of her work online. @julia.cripps1 | soulart.live

Andy Dalgleish grew up in Northumberland, beside the River Tyne, and now teaches history in West Cornwall. Wild nature and landscape often feature in his poems, which have appeared in a number of publications, including *Magma*. Andy won the Leeds Peace Poetry Prize in 2022.

Elaine Desmond is from near Skibbereen in Ireland. Her poetry has appeared in the *Irish Chair of Poetry Anthology*, *Hive*, and *Ogham Stone*, among others. Elaine has been listed or commended in various awards, including the UK's National Poetry Competition and the Fish Poetry Prize. She holds an MA in Creative Writing and was mentored by poet Grace Wells at Munster Literature Centre.

Kristina Diprose co-runs the 'Rhubarb at the Triangle' open mic in Shipley, West Yorkshire, and co-edited its anthologies *Un/Forced* and *Seconds*. Shortlisted in the Ginkgo Prize and Leeds Poetry Festival competitions, she was an Ilkley Lit Fest 2023 'New Northern Poet'. *Thin Spells,* her debut pamphlet of ecopoetry, is forthcoming from Black Cat Poetry in 2025. @kristinadiprose

Silvia El Helo is a London-based artist and translator with Jordanian and Slovakian roots. Her poems have appeared in numerous online magazines and, most recently, her work was included in the collection *We Wrote in Symbols: Love and Lust by Arab Women Writers* (Saqi Books, London) and the anthology *We Call to the Eye & the Night* (Persea Books, New York).

Fhen M studied World Literature at Eastern Visayas State University in the Philippines and played an active role in a creative writing workshop. His poem 'Uyasan' (or 'Toy') was published in the book *Pinili:15 Years of Lamiraw*. His English verse 'Lighthouse' and other poems have appeared in the *Poetica* anthology series published by Clarendon House. @poet_of_virtue_and_sin | Facebook: Fhen Em | diaryof404.wordpress.com

Tessa Foley's debut poetry collection *Chalet Between Thick Ears* and follow-up *What Sort of Bird are You?* were published by Live Canon. She had previously won that publisher's International Poetry Prize and has been commended in a number of other competitions. Now working on her third collection *Try to Find Me*, Tessa works at the Poetry School in London (*so that's where you might find her* ☺ *– ed.*). @tessafoleypoet | tessafoley.com

Sarah Garland is a published photographic artist based in the UK. The drive behind her practice is the search for beauty and 'essence' in the hidden jewels of the natural and urban world around her. Her hope is to create images that inspire people to think and feel deeply in their response – and find connections with things 'beyond themselves'. @sarahheartsoul

Frances Gaudiano is a writer and a veterinary nurse. She has published two novels, *The Listener* and *The Home Straight*. Her poetry and short stories have appeared in a variety of online and print journals and she is the author of a textbook on Veterinary Dermatology. @francesgaudiano | francesgaudiano.substack.com

Anita Gracey has been published in *Poetry Ireland Review*, the *Washing Windows – Irish Women Write Poetry* series, *Abridged*, *The Honest Ulsterman*, *Poetry NI*, *The Poets' Republic*, *Fly on the Wall*, *Blue Nib*, *Culture* and *The Poetry Jukebox*. Shortlisted in several competitions, most recently the Skylight 47 Mentoring Programme, Anita currently participates in creative writing workshops at the Irish Writers Centre.

Robin Green is a largely self-taught photographer, often employing experimental techniques to capture images of the natural world – such as multiple exposures, macro-magnification and infrared lighting – using a mixture of modern, vintage and self-modified equipment. He also works as a sound professional in television and film. @greenandbaileyphoto

Alex Hadwen-Bennett is a creative botanical photographer based in Cambridgeshire, who employs a light box in his work to bring out the fine details in plants. 'Dazzle', the cover image for this volume of FLORA/FAUNA, was inspired by the symbolic use of the zebra to represent rare conditions such as Ehlers-Danlos Syndrome, from which Alex himself suffers. @alexhbdesigns

Jane Hanson is an English teacher, artist and poet who lives on the island of Ischia in Southern Italy. Her work has been published in anthologies by The Wee Sparrow Poetry Press. An animal lover giving refuge to many abandoned animals, she also campaigns for human rights causes focused on the homeless and refugees. Her paintings, poems and photographs are inspired by nature and wildlife.

Jaqi Holland is a poet living north of Boston, Massachusetts, who holds an MA in Writing & Publishing from Emerson College. Her work has appeared in *The Christian Science Monitor*, *The Ekphrastic Review*, *Brevity & Echo*, *Humana Obscura* and *Plant People: an Anthology of Environmental Artists*. jaqiholland.com

Samantha Hoover is a visual artist based in West Texas. She finds inspiration everywhere, from famous artworks to neighbourhood walks and her life experiences. She has a passion for seeking the extraordinary in everyday life and sharing it with the world. Her mediums of choice are photography (specifically black-and-white compositions) and watercolour painting. @s.s.designco

Anthony Ibuaka is an artist passionate about the beauty, elegance and vibrancy of photography. He aims to create timeless, expressive works that compel, communicate, explore and uplift, appreciating or celebrating his chosen subjects. Nature is among several things that inspire his work – in which he embraces natural light. @anthonyibuakaphotography | @anthonaka

Mary Beth Kaplan lives in Northern Indiana with her husband, three beautiful kids and two fur babies. Her work has been seen in several anthology series and a greetings card collection. She is a small shop proprietor who loves listening to The Beatles, gardening and anything vintage. @the_paperbackmama | mantrasandcoffee.substack.com

David Lewis has been writing for over thirty years. His poems capture brief encounters with birds, trees, and silence in the winter landscapes of the Welsh Marches. He also writes books about his native Liverpool and works as a school librarian.

Sylvie Jane Lewis writes poetry and fiction, and has an MPhil in English from Cambridge. Her work has featured in *Ink Sweat & Tears*, *Spellbinder* and *Spinozablue*. Recently, her poetry appeared in *Smashed Peaches* (2023), an anthology of women and nonbinary writers on surviving violence. @sylviejanelewis

Jane Lovell lives in North Devon on the edge of the Valley of Rocks. Her work focuses on our relationship with the planet and its wildlife. She is widely published in the UK and US and has recently won the Ginkgo and Rialto Nature & Place Poetry Prizes. Her new collection, *On Earth, as it is,* is published by Hazel Press. janelovellpoetry.co.uk

Elizabeth Lukács Chesla writes, edits and teaches from the suburbs of Philadelphia, where her photo in this volume was taken. Her award-winning historical fiction novella, *You Cannot Forbid the Flower*, was published by Tolsun Books in 2023. She serves as an assistant fiction editor for *Consequence Forum* and on the board of the Transformative Language Arts Network. elizabethchesla.com

Chas MacKinnon is an Irish writer. Born in Belfast, he's lived all over the UK and a few other places beyond. Currently, he teaches English at a secondary school in Yorkshire. When he's not doing that, he can be found looking for poetry in the prosaic and for stories hiding in plain sight.

Frankie Martins is a 16-year-old poet from Surrey, currently studying for his GCSEs, and has been twice commended as a Foyle Young Poet (2022 and 2023). He is also a keen artist and believes this brings a highly visual element to his writing. He finds inspiration in everything from summer holidays to existential dread. @fronksnotdead.

Holly McKenna is an emerging poet from central Scotland and poet-in-residence for Glasgow University's 'Women in Law' project. She has previously been published in *Myth and Lore*, *The Levatio*, *Honey and Lime*, *Vita Brevis* and *Qmunicate*. Holly's work combines the poetic with the unexpected, weaving poetry from pain. She hopes to someday release a collection of her own.

Trish Morgan is a designer with 30+ years' experience, currently designing magazines for Butterfly Conservation West Midlands, amongst others. Since discovering a passion for photography at art school, she has found inspiration in nature and her rural surroundings, developing an eye for all things quirky and unusual. @morgancreative_ | morgancreative.carbonmade.com | Flickr: squizzel2013

Paul Morris has been a practising fine artist for over thirty years with a long exhibiting history. His first book, *A Toby in the Lane, A History of London's East End Markets*, was published by The History Press in 2014. Now living in Hertfordshire, Paul pursues his love of street photography in London and coastal towns, together with English landscape photography. @paulmorris177 | paulmorris.photography

Laura Muetzelfeldt is a writer from Glasgow who has been published in such journals as *The International Literary Quarterly* and *New Writing Scotland*. After an MLitt degree in Creative Writing at the University of Glasgow, she worked as an English Teacher for seven years. Laura recently completed a PhD in Creative Writing at the University of St Andrews and is currently working on her debut novel.

Navila Nahid is a landscape photographer and writer based in New York. This is her first publication. Her work can be found on her Instagram accounts and website. @whimsyinthedetail | @navilanahidpoetry | navila85.com

Michele Noble is an artist and poet now living in East Yorkshire. Places in which she has lived have always influenced her written and visual work. Her two poems here relate to walking on the Pennines above Stainforth, and her back garden in West Ayton, near Scarborough. She is now working on her first collection of poetry. @michelenobleartist | michelenobleartist.co.uk

Joseph Nutman writes the majority of his poetry whilst rambling around Hertfordshire trying to find pockets of wild in the fields around his home. His poetic voice resides in the tension between nature, psyche, society and personal history. His work has appeared in issues of *Spelt*, *Shearsman*, *Sunday Mornings at the River* and *Poetry Cove*. @joseph_nutman

Tim Paddock plays with a creative imagination in different media including fine art, photography and writing, inventions and community development. His focus is on interactions between perception and interpretation – always inspired by the nature of our surroundings. When not making, he might be surfing or fishing. See his colourfield abstractions on Instagram. @timpaddockart

Andrea Penner has published poetry in anthologies, chapbooks and literary magazines, most recently *Neologism* and *Sky Island Journal*. Her second book, *Rabbit Sun, Lotus Moon* (Mercury HeartLink, 2017) was a poetry finalist for an Arizona/New Mexico book award. From her Albuquerque home, she serves up poetry, creative non-fiction and memoir in her Substack newsletter, *In Our Own Ink*.

Akash Pillai is an emerging fiction writer and poet. He holds a first-class BA in English Literature and Creative Writing from Swansea University and is now pursuing postgraduate studies in Creative Writing at the University of Leicester. His poetry illuminates the experience of growing up within a minority community in Britain. Akash is currently crafting his debut fiction manuscript. TikTok: @ahashi04

Helen Pletts has four times been shortlisted for the Bridport Poetry Prize (2018, 2019, 2022 and 2023), twice longlisted in The Rialto Nature & Place Competition (2018 and 2022), longlisted for the Ginkgo Prize (2019), and longlisted in the National Poetry Competition (2022). She placed 2nd in the Plaza Prose Poetry Prize 2022-23. @helen.pletts | helenpletts.com

Alena Pollitt is a queer artist and photographer from Washington DC. She enjoys travel and street photography – capturing life's uncontrived beauty, with a focus on finding elegance in the textures and contrasts of her surroundings. With deep curiosity and attention to detail, Alena aims to tell simple, authentic stories through her lens. @alenapollitphoto | alenapollitt.com

Hylain Rackley is a haiku poet with a published book, *Simple Joys* (2023), under the pen-name of Hylain Wright, and an upcoming volume called *Love Letters To Myself* (2024). Her haiku have appeared in the anthologies *Poets of the Promise* and *Harmonic Verse*. A certified yogini, she is an advocate for mindfulness and life-long learning. Hylain lives in North Carolina with her husband and two daughters.

Joe Rainbow was born in 1976 and spent his formative years in a rural farm setting in Cornwall, near the beautiful Helford river. He studied Painting at Cardiff University, going on to teach Art at a Cornish secondary school. Joe has photographed the landscape since the age of 16, now focusing on the less-told stories of the Lizard peninsula and beyond. @joe.w.rainbow | joerainbowphotography.com

Cindy Rinne creates poetry and fibre art in San Bernardino, California. Her poems have appeared in anthologies, art exhibits and dance performances. Cindy is the author of several books: *Dancing Through the Fire Door* (Nauset Press), *The Feather Ladder* (Picture Show Press) and more. Her poetry has appeared in *The Closed Eye Open, Verse-Virtual* and *Mythos Magazine* among others. @fiberverse | fiberverse.com

M T Ross began writing poetry consistently in 2023 when she joined a creative writing class, challenging herself to try new things. A passion was sparked – fulfilling her primary school teacher's prediction that she'd be a writer one day. Her poem 'My North Star' is a proud reflection of her Northern roots – which she hopes will resonate with you, wherever you may call home.

Susan Sancomb is a photographer and graphic designer based in Rhode Island, New England. She is inspired by the natural world – specifically bodies of water – capturing their myriad qualities in unique and abstract ways for her black-and-white series 'Drifting East'. Susan spends much of her free time hiking, bike riding, painting and kayaking. @susansancombphoto | sancombphotography.com

Kelly Schulze is a New York State-based photographer who grew up beside the Hudson and Croton rivers, giving her a love of the great outdoors. Her photography – using natural light, texture, pattern and perspective – captures abstract and intimate nature. Her work has been published in *Humana Obscura* and exhibited locally. @kellyschulze_photography | kellyschulzephotography.com

Andi Sherridan Howley is a chef and photography enthusiast who spends their time travelling the world onboard cruise ships. By day they work as a chef de partie, while downtime is spent behind the lens of a camera, capturing images from their travels. @andi_sherridan.photography | Facebook: Andi sherridan photography

Di Slaney runs the Nottinghamshire livestock sanctuary Manor Farm Charitable Trust and independent publisher Candlestick Press. Winner of The Plough Poetry Prize 2022, she has been broadcast and anthologised – as well as highly commended in the Forward Prize 2016 and Bridport Prize 2020. Her collections *Reward for Winter* and *Herd Queen* are available from Valley Press. @di_slaney | candlestickpress.co.uk

Lorri Smalls is a content writer and author living in Bloomfield, New Jersey, who discovered a passion for photography in 2021 – a refreshing break from the often-routine work of content development which helped keep her creative spirit alive. She considers it a blessing to have the opportunity to tell stories of everyday life through photography. @widow40 | LinkedIn: lorri-smalls-9026b4133

Jamie Smart, aged 8 (yes, eight) is an award-winning nature photographer, with a passion for shooting wildlife. She first picked up her dad's camera and began taking images as a 6-year-old – progressing to become, within a couple of years, the youngest ever RSPCA Photographer of the Year (2023). Her wish is to help people fall in love with nature. @eagle_eyed_grl | @eagle_eyed_girl | eagleeyedgirl.co.uk

Jake Spencer is a London-based fashion photographer whose work focuses on communicating a strong and clear connection with the subject. Although his subjects are primarily people, he also uses his eye for composition to capture nature and street images whilst regularly out and about in the UK. @jakespencerphoto | jakespencerphoto.co.uk

Emma Steele's photography attempts to find the alien in the ordinary. Her mostly long-exposure landscapes create a serene yet unsettling world, where human-made objects – sea defences, beach huts, traffic cones – intertwine with natural surroundings to transcend their everyday reality. Some might say that, living in Norfolk as she does, the otherworldly is second nature to her! @machinecreative

Holly Stewart is a self-taught photographer, focusing primarily on landscapes and wildlife. Growing up on the Devon/Cornwall border, Dartmoor National Park prompted and developed her interest in nature and, despite moving to Kent to complete her formal Architectural education, Holly remains focused on living creatures and the wider environment in her work. @winding.lens

Lisa Stone began her working life in publishing, then taught English for many years. She is now a wellbeing and mental health coach and spends as much time as possible writing. Following long-time involvement with humanitarian charities, her poetry tends to focus on social, environmental, mental health and displacement issues – aiming to promote wider awareness. @patchworktatty.

Jessica Taggart Rose is a writer and editor concerned with humanity, nature and how the two interact. She has been published in the *Letters to the Earth* and the *Green Ink: Wild Weather* anthologies, *Confluence Magazine* and a range of other zines. She's a founding member of Poets for the Planet and one half of the 'Promenade' performance duo. She lives in Margate, Kent. @jessicataggartrose

Samantha Terrell is a Pushcart-nominated poet with multiple 5-star collections, who writes at home in Upstate New York. Her poems have been widely anthologised in publications such as *Dark Winter Lit*, *Green Ink Poetry*, *In Parentheses*, *Misfit Magazine*, *Open Journal of Arts & Letters*, *Poetry Quarterly*, *Red Ogre Review* and *Wildfire Words* among others. @honestypoetrybysamamtha | samanthaterrell.com

Marco Tiboni is an Italian photographer living and working in London. He gradually discovered his passion for photography working first as a videographer and then as a graphic designer. Although his true love is travel-portraiture, wildlife and landscapes are also central to his work, which aims to freeze and preserve moments of life in all its many facets. @marcotiboni86

Erica Vanstone is a mom, CEO, author, poet, and avid coffee drinker living in Philadelphia. She started out as a filmmaker, with a degree from NYU Film, yet found her way to sports management. She now spends her free time foil fencing, running, and fostering good will between her two dogs and one highly opinionated cat. @ericavanstone | ericavanstone.com

Christian Ward is a UK-based poet with recent work in *Acumen*, *Dreich*, *Dream Catcher*, *Dodging the Rain* and *Canary*. He was longlisted for the 2023 Aurora Prize for Writing, shortlisted for the 2023 Ironbridge Poetry Competition and 2023 Aesthetica Creative Writing Award, and won the 2023 Cathalbui Poetry Competition. @fighting_cancer_with_poetry

Joy Wassell Timms is a nature-loving writer based in Manchester. Two collections of her poems were published in 2022: *SHOUT* and *Word Hoards*. Other work has been published in *The North*, *Orbis* and *Obsessed with Pipework*. With an MA from Manchester Metropolitan University, she is Writer in Residence at Burnage Library and runs Open Mics there. @batwob | joywasselltimms.co.uk

Natalie Wilson is a mountain leader and adventure travel guide. Recently Natalie set out on a new adventure, that of combining her passion for the outdoors with her love of words. Now her travel writing and poetry are starting to make their way into the world – and she is working on her first book. @adventuresafoot | adventuresafoot.co.uk

David Wright has been a documentary photographer since the 1970s, spending most of his life on immersive long-term projects. His 1980s/90s series about the rural, west coast of Ireland provides a unique insight into a way of life that has largely disappeared. His more recent work, 'Modern Tribes of England', documents groups ranging from goths to morris dancers. @davidgilbertwright | davidwright.photography

Gaby Zak is a nature and landscape photographer. She has exhibited at Oxfordshire Artweeks and at The Base Greenham, and has had work published in magazines such as *Amateur Photographer*, *Outdoor Photography* and *Conker Nature*. Her favourite place to shoot is Dumfries and Galloway, focusing on its vast landscapes and natural beauty. @gzphoto_ | gzak46.wixsite.com/portfolio

Zhou Yang is an artist using the medium of photography, whose work explores the themes of memory, cultural heritage and myth. Her ongoing 'Faërie' project focuses on traditional Chinese literati gardens and shows them as a form of spatial imagination where it is possible to escape mortality. This is also the starting point of her current PhD research at Birmingham City University. @zyfotos2 | zyfotos.viewbook.com

BEV CLOUGH: *Never Forget*